Carving the Old Woman's Shoe

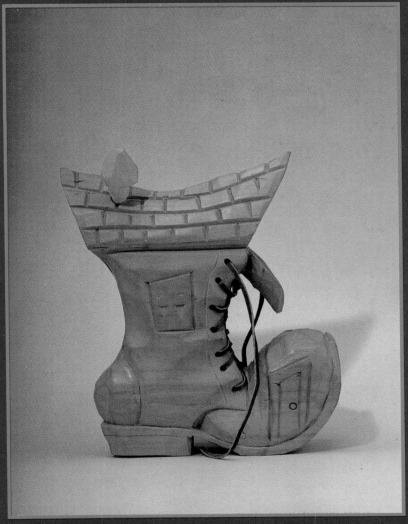

with Larry Green

77 Lower Valley Road, Atglen, PA 19310

Art work by Mike Altman
Photography by Steve Smith

Dedication

To Myra, my wife, and Jeff, my son who are my best critics. To Steve Smith for his hard work and advice on the book.

Acknowledgements

Thanks to Mike Altman for his creative drawings and to Mary Lape and Brandi Lawrence for their help. Thanks to Deborah Berkley who wanted to help but was too busy. And a special thanks to Professor Ron Wheeler who makes sure my English is correct.

Copyright © 1994 by Larry Green

Artwork by Mike Altman
Photography by Steve Smith

Printed in China
ISBN: 0-88740-603-3

We are interested in hearing from authors with book ideas on related topics.

Published by Schiffer Publishing Ltd.
77 Lower Valley Road
Atglen, PA 19310
Please write for a free catalog.
This book may be purchased from the publisher.
Please include $2.95 postage.
Try your bookstore first.

Contents

Introduction

Ly Green
"HAPPY CARVING"

One of the unexpected joys of writing my first book, *Carving Boots and Shoes*, has been developing friendships with fellow carvers. Folks who read the book have called, sent photos and mailed samples of their shoe carvings; some have even stopped at the woodcarving shop at Dollywood to talk about their carving experiences.

Since I started carving shoes, one shoe that has continued to hold my attention has been the shoe house from the nursery rhyme, "THE OLD WOMAN IN THE SHOE." I have made several attempts at carving that shoe. In my first attempt, I carved a boot and then glued a carved roof on the top. The result was not good. After that failure, I developed a new pattern and made another attempt. Still not satisfied with this effort, I worked on several other patterns until finally producing the one in this book. Pattern development takes time. I hope you have as much joy carving the shoe as I had in developing it.

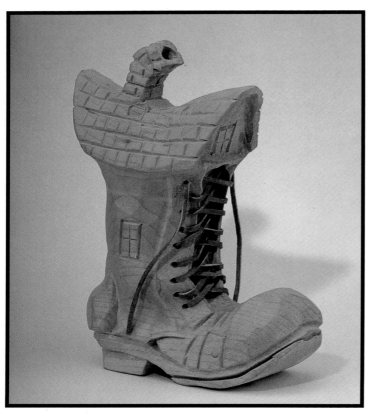

Mike Altman has created our concept of the Old Woman. Since, the poem doesn't seem to portray her in a very good light we decided to create a more positive image. We would like to refer to her as a wise woman. She is going to assist in the carving of the shoe. Her name is Mrs. Merry Whittler. I decided to write my own poem.

getting started

Most of the carving will be completed with a knife. I use a couple different size blades on all of my carvings. The larger thicker blade at the top is for the rough out work. The two smaller blades are for detail work. If you only have one knife, then that's what you need to use. My knives, made by Ken Helvie in Indiana, have tungsten carbon steel blades. The handles are made of Pakkawood, a selected hardwood veneer which has been vacuum impregnated with color dyes and phenolic resins. The veneer is bonded together under pressure and high temperature to form a multi-layer laminate.

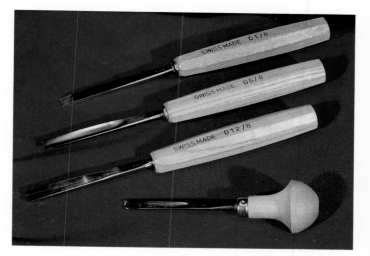

A variety of gouges will be helpful. I especially like to use an 8mm No. 12 V-parting tool, an 8mm No. 5 gouge, and an 8mm chisel for some of cuts on the shoe. A 5mm No. 9 palm gouge will help make the cuts on the windows and an 10mm No. 7 palm gouge (not pictured) will aid work on the tongue.

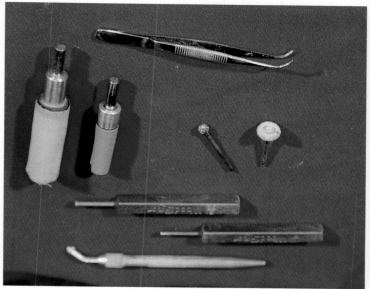

Some additional items that are helpful would be a pattern wheel, curved tweezers, two styles of course carbide Kutzall™ burrs (one flat and one round). A sheet of 220 grit or finer sandpaper (not pictured) or a cushioned sanding drum with 220 grit paper are very helpful. A Scotch-Brite™ pad (not pictured) will also be helpful.

A wood carver's safety glove is helpful as well. You can find one in most wood carving supply catalogs. It's a good investment.

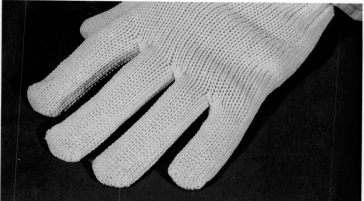

The Patterns

The shoe is cut from a 2" basswood board with the grain running from toe to heel. The pattern is pictured actual size. If you reduce the pattern by 50%, you might want to use 1 1/4" wood. The extra 1/4" would give you a little more wood with which to work. Don't be afraid to experiment with pattern enlargements or reductions.

The yard pattern is placed on a 3/4" basswood board with the grain running the length of the yard.

Grain

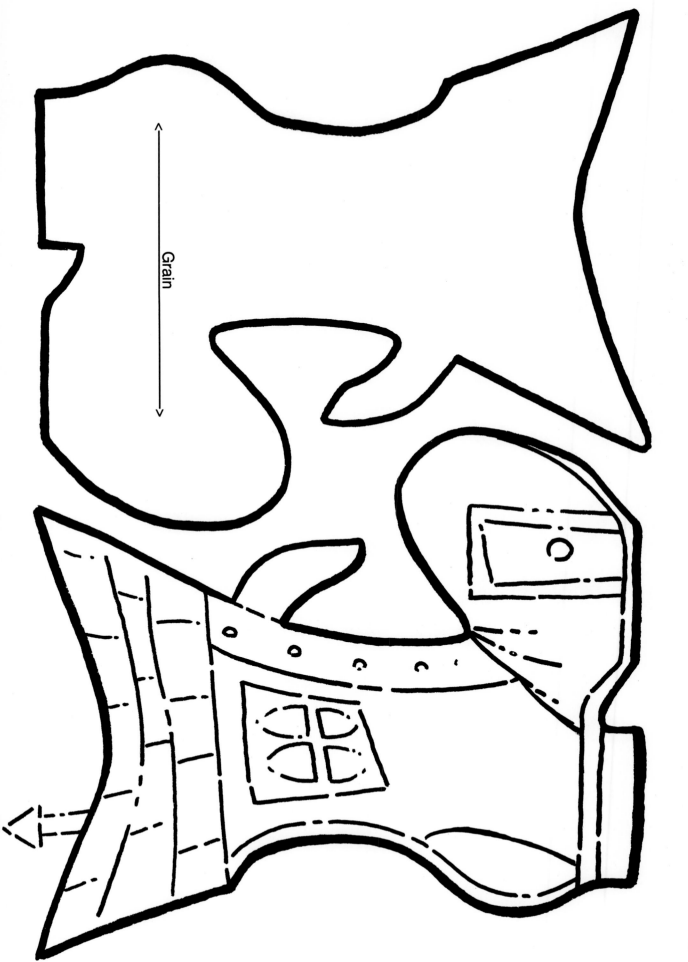

Grain

1.

I suggest the use of a carving glove just in case the knife takes on a mind of it's own.

2.

Do not become so focused on carving that you forget about your hand placement. Keep your free hand out of the path of the knife or gouge. Nothing can end your carving fun quicker than a cut.

3.

Before you make a cut pictured in the book, you might want to look ahead to the next couple of pictures. In fact, looking back a few pictures can be helpful as well.

4.

When using a bit, burr, or a sanding drum in a drill, make sure it is inserted properly and firmly locked in place. You should wear safety glasses or goggles for eye protection when using power equipment.

5.

Give the carving your own personality. The book is designed to give you the basics of carving the shoe. Add cuts, detail and design ideas to make it your own.

Carving the SHOE

You are viewing 3 stages of carving the shoe. The first stage is the band sawed blank. The second is the shaped shoe with detail added. The third is the finished work.

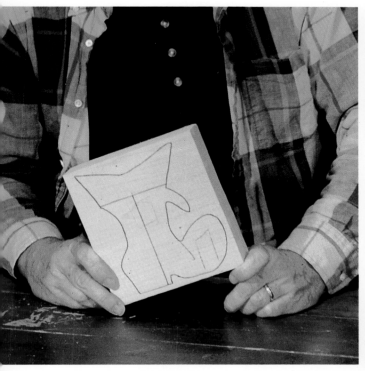

Use carbon paper to trace your pattern on a 2" thick basswood board with the grain running toe to heel. Cut your pattern out with a band saw.

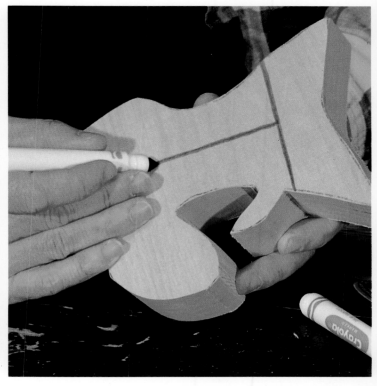

Draw a center line on the front, back, roof, sole and sides. Add the eave line as well.

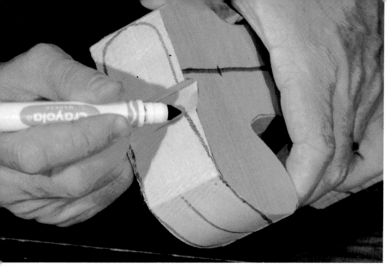

Draw on the heel and sole. I am carving a left shoe.

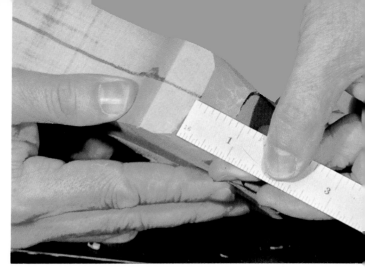

The completed cuts.

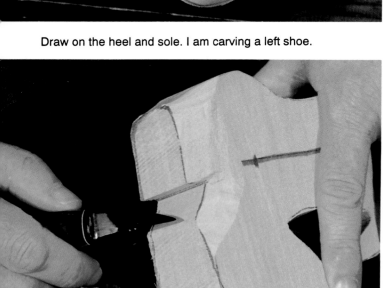

Shape the instep and heel.

Remove wood to the sole lines on the front and side of the toe.

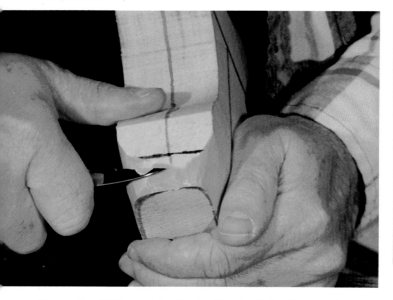

Draw a line 3/4" up on the back of the heel. Cut the wood away from the heel line to that line.

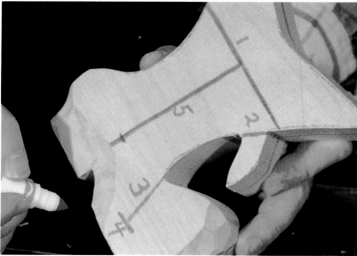

Your shoe should already have the center line (5) and eave line (1). If not, draw them at this time. Now draw 3 lines on both sides of the shoe. Lines 2 & 3 set what I call the "lace walls". Line 4 is a stop cut reference line.

use a carving glove!

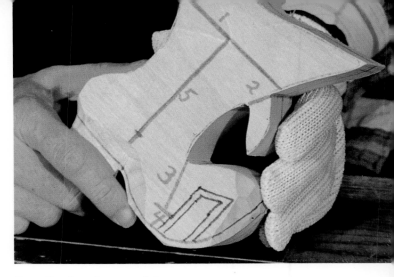

Draw the door frame and door.

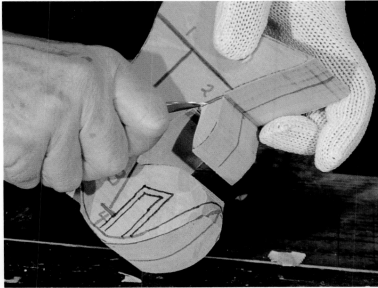

Incise line 2. Repeat on the other side.

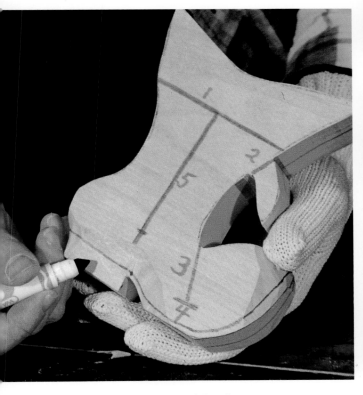

Draw the heel and sole line around the shoe.

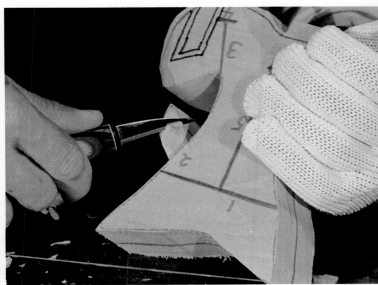

Remove some wood back to line 2. Cut in approximately 1/4".
Repeat on the other side.

The completed cuts.

Repeat the process on the other side. Since there is no door on this side, you can remove more wood on the toe.

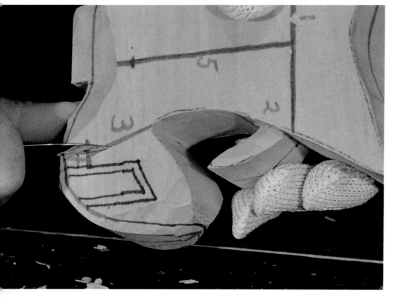

Incise line 3 stopping at line 4. Repeat on the other side.

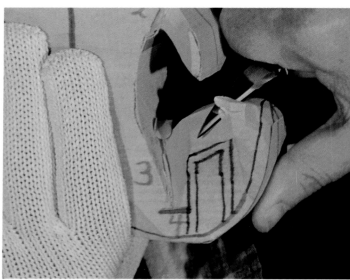

Round the toe to your liking. BE CAREFUL not to cut into the lines of the door frame. The shoe should drop away from the door on the top and sides. Do not cut off the sole lines on the toe.

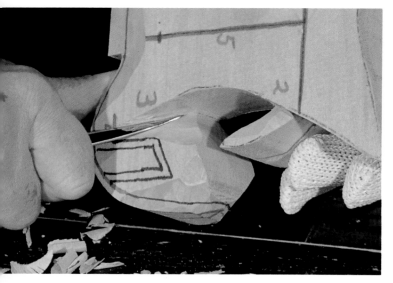

Cut wood away to line 3. DO NOT cut into the outline of the door frame. The wood needs to fall away from the door frame to line 3.

The completed cuts.

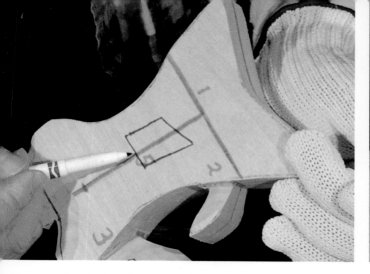

Draw on the window. Repeat on the other side.

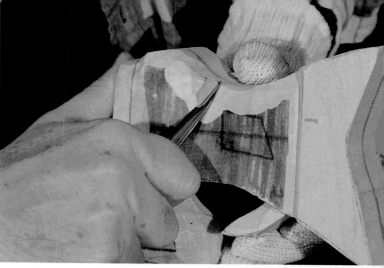

Now, we need to turn our attention to rounding the shoe. I have begun to contour the side of the shoe. I added some blue color to help the cuts stand out. You don't need to do this to your shoe. The goal is to round the shoe from the center line on the side to the center line on the back.

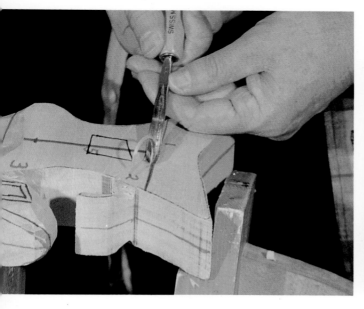

Clamp the shoe in a vise or use a method of your choosing to secure the shoe. Run your v-tool along the roof eave line. I'm using an 8mm No. 12 V-parting tool. Make sure that the v-tool is angled so that you are only removing wood from the shoe rather than the roof. Make several shallow cuts rather than one big deep cut. You want to cut about 1/4" deep. Repeat on the other side.

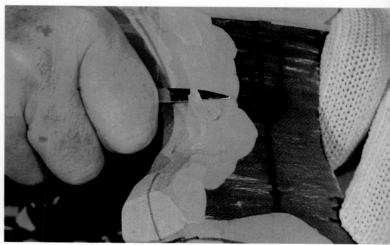

The continued rounding of the shoe toward the center line on the back. Be Careful that you don't cut into the window. The shoe needs to drop away from the window.

The completed cuts.

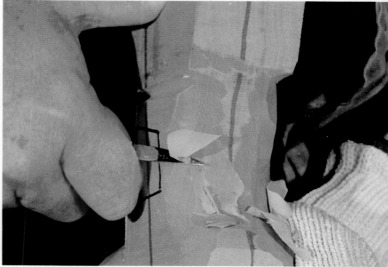

Repeat this process on the other side.

The completed rounding of the back.

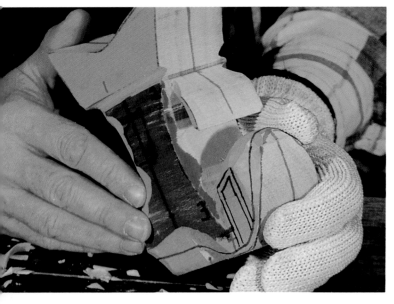

Draw on the lace walls. The pink colored area will be removed. Repeat on the other side.

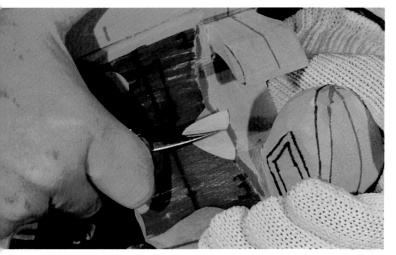

Make several scooping cuts tapering the wood from the lace wall to the window and center line. Repeat this process up and down the length of the lace wall. Do not make any scooping cuts lower than line four. Repeat other side.

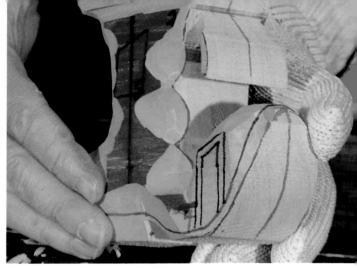

The completed cuts. This picture shows you how I have stopped my scooping cuts right at line 4.

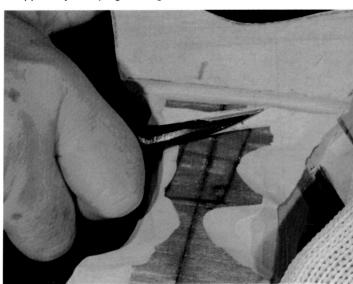

Taper the shoe into the roof eave line. The wood should drop away from the window to the eave line. Repeat on the other side.

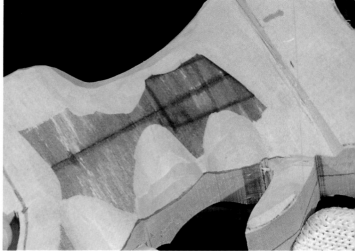

The completed tapering. You might want to look back a couple of pictures for reference.

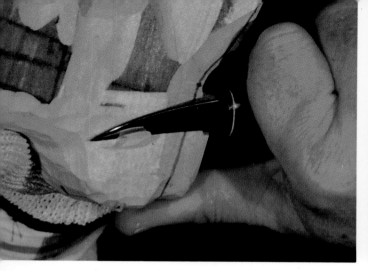

Complete the rounding of the shoe at this time. You can see that I am removing the remaining blue color. As I do this, I'm contouring and rounding the shoe.

Make four stop cuts just above and below the horizontal center line on the window. I have used a marker to show their location.

Run your v-tool on the lines of the window frame. Repeat on the other side.

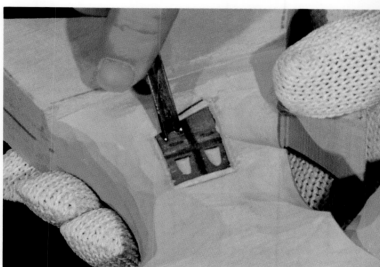

Use a 5mm No. 9 gouge to cut back to the stop cuts. This cut shapes a window pane. Repeat the process on the other window.

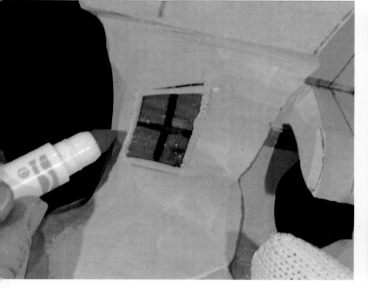

Draw center lines on the window.

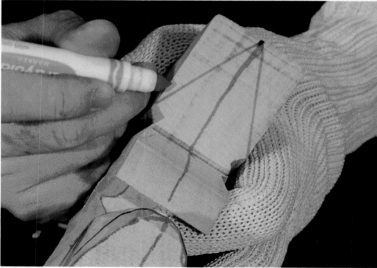

Draw the roof lines on the front and back.

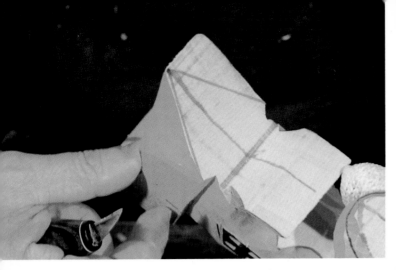

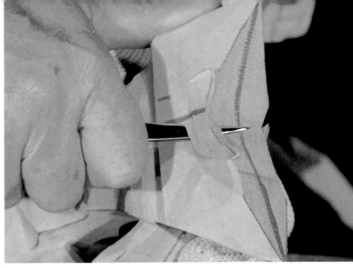

Taper the wood from the eave line to the roof center line.

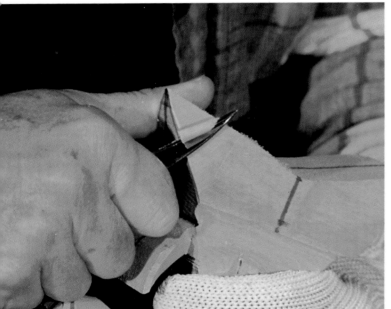

Cut the wood away to the lines.

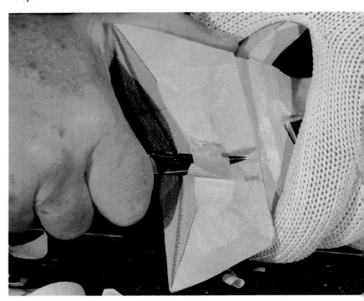

Repeat on the other side.

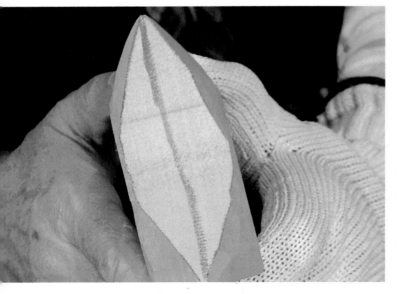

I have outlined the wood left remaining after the previous cuts. This wood will need to be removed.

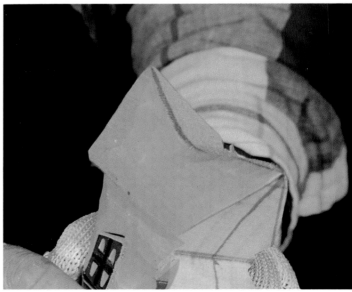

The completed work on one side of the roof.

Draw on the individual shingles.

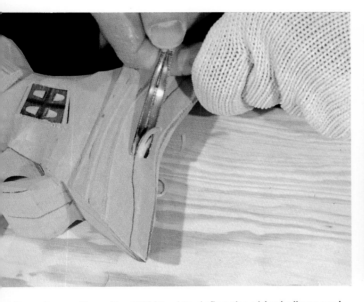

I'm using an 8mm No. 12 V-tool to define the shingle lines and a c-clamp to hold the shoe while I make the cuts. I place a thin scrap of wood under the clamp so as not to mire the carving. The clamp allows me to use two hands and thus, I think, give me better control of the v-tool.

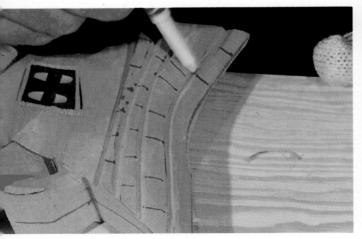

Remove the shoe from the c-clamp and draw on the individual shingles.

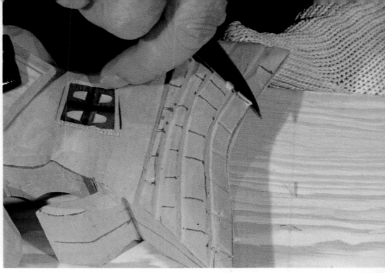

To define the individual shingles, use your v-tool or make v-cuts with your knife on the lines. Personal preference should be your guide as to whether you use a v-tool or knife.

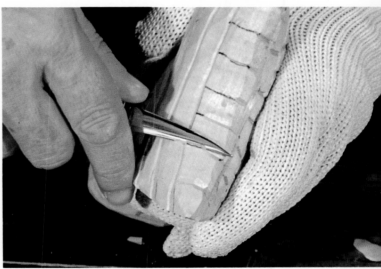

Add shingle lines across the top of the roof and then use your v-tool or make v-cuts with your knife.

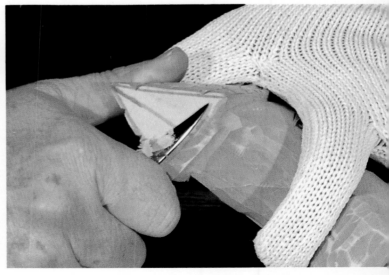

Use your knife to remove the saw marks from the eaves on the front and back.

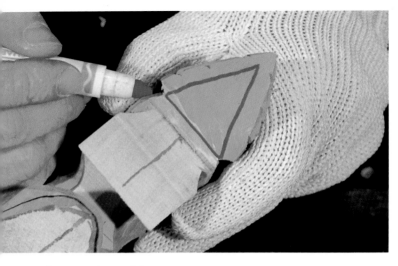

Draw on the roof lines.

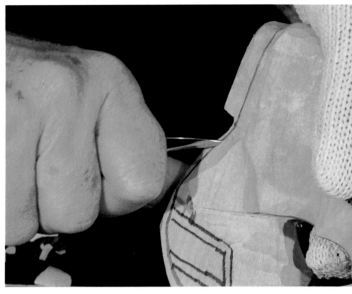

Deeply incise the sole line completely around the shoe.

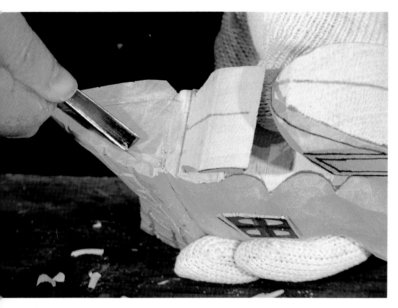

Run your v-tool down their length both front and back. Remember to think about hand placement.

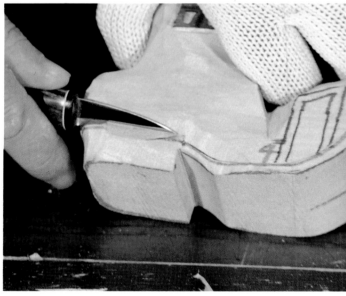

Trim back to the incised line from the top of the shoe. This cut sets the shape between the sole and the body of the shoe. The deeper the angle of the cut the wider the sole.

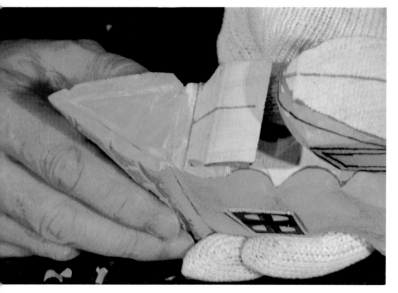

The completed cuts.

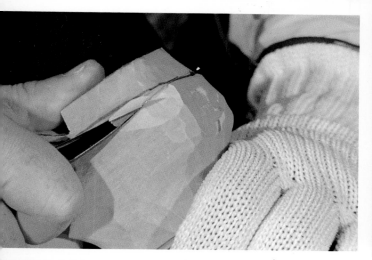

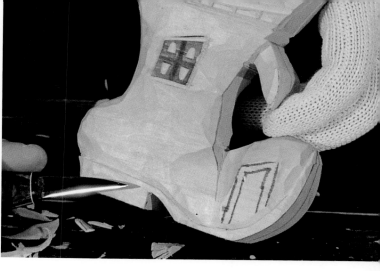

The completed removal of wood around the sole.

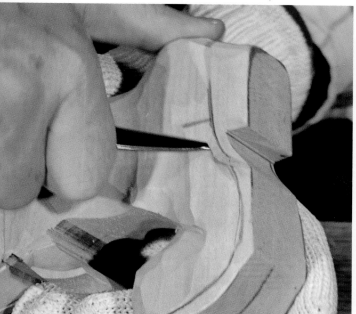

Continue to work your way around the shoe.

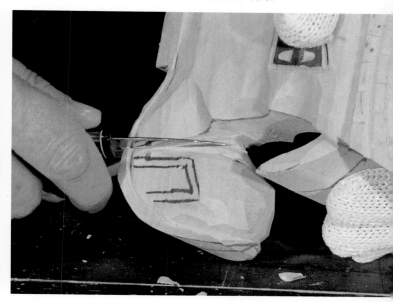

Add wrinkles by making v-cuts with the knife. Extend some of the wrinkles to the sole. Repeat on the other side.

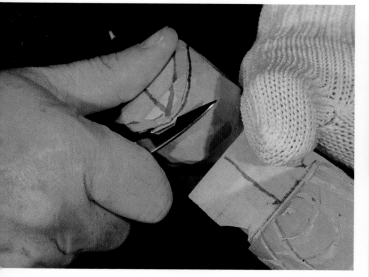

Be careful as you cut back to the incised line on the toe. Because the grain runs off the end of the toe, it will be very easy to cut completely through the sole.

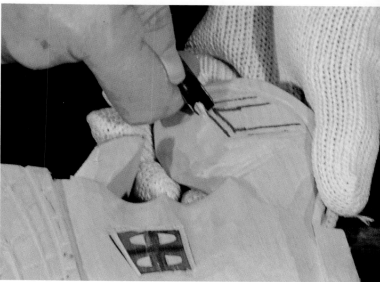

Run your v-tool on the lines of the door frame.

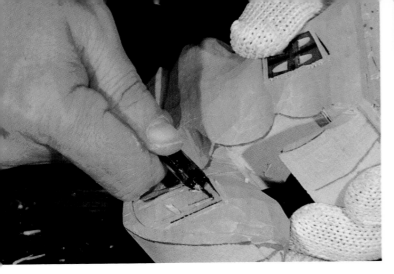

Run your v-tool on the lines of the door.

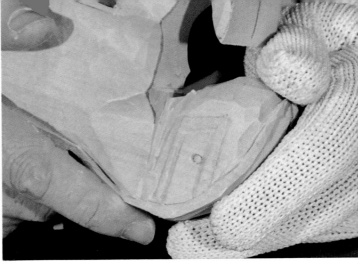

The completed v-tool and eye punch work on the door.

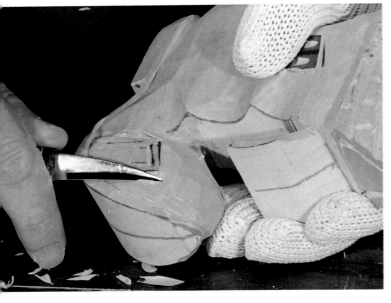

Use your knife to clean up any v-tool cuts which extend past the door frame.

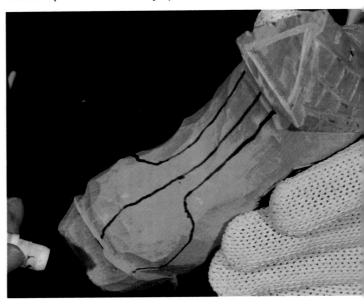

Draw a center line on the back of the shoe and then draw the seam cover.

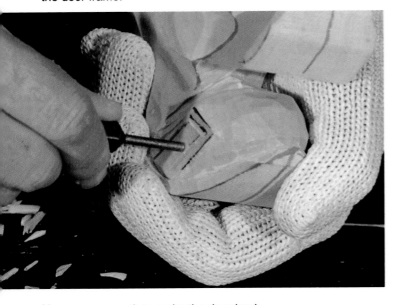

Use an eye-punch to make the door knob.

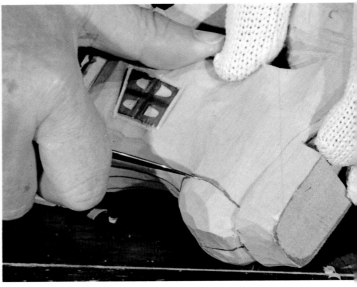

Incise the line.

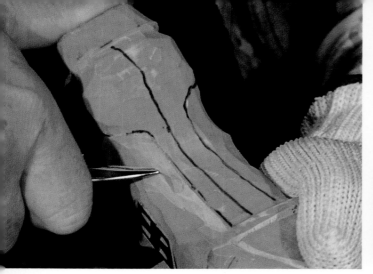

Cut back to the incised line.

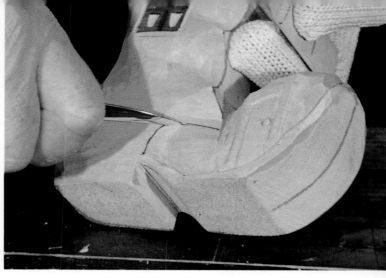

Deeply incise the line.

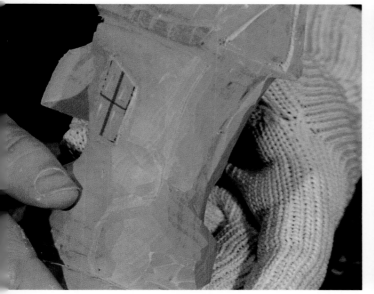

The complete cuts.

Trim back to the incised line. This may take several cuts to get this wood removed.

Draw a line from the lace wall to the sole. Repeat on the other side.

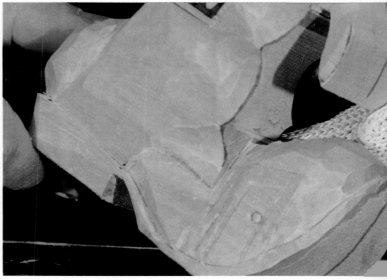

The completed cuts.

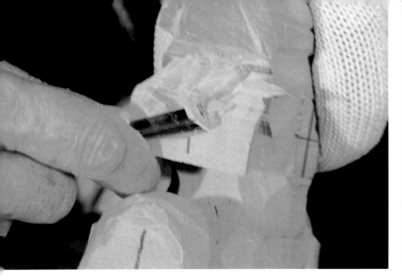

Scoop out the tongue. Don't apply a lot of pressure on the tongue. You don't want to break it off. I'm using a 10mm No. 7 palm gouge.

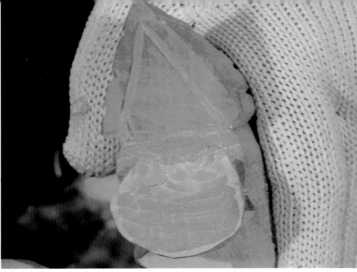

The finished top of the tongue.

The completed scooping out of the tongue.

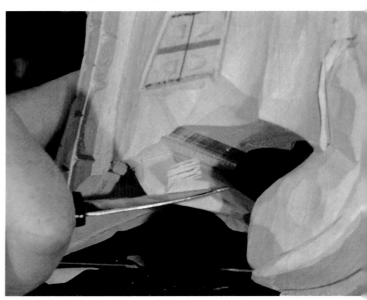

Make the tongue a uniform thickness by removing wood from the bottom of the tongue. Don't apply a lot of pressure on the tongue or you might end up holding it in your hand.

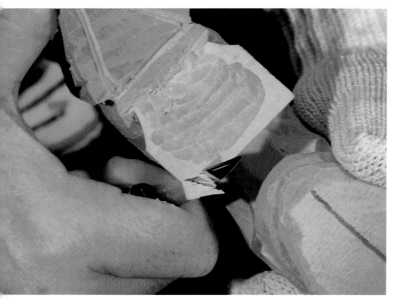

Round the tongue by cutting off the saw marks.

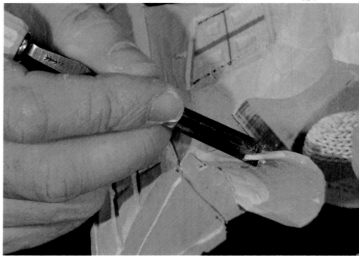

I'm using a chisel to define the edge of the tongue. Your knife will work as well.

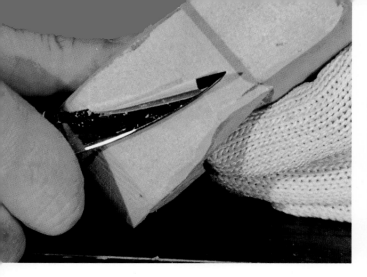

Clean away the saw marks on the bottom of the sole and heel.

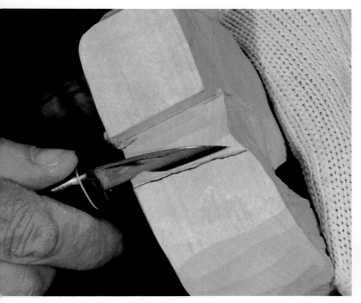

Add a half sole by incising a line across the sole and trimming back to it.

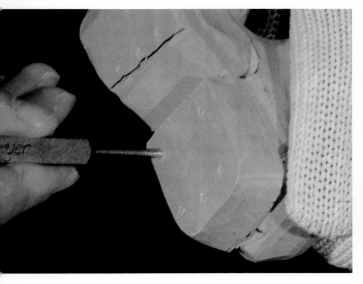

Add nails heads to the heel and half sole with an eye punch or twist the point of your knife.

Take a break!

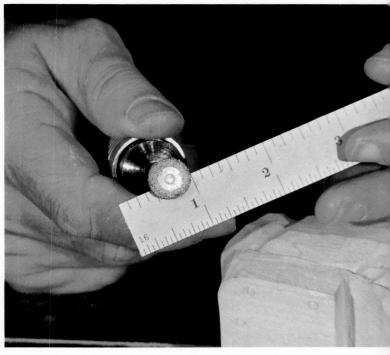

I'm going to use a Foredom™ flexible shaft tool and 1/2" by 1/8" Kutzall™ carbide burr to remove the wood between the lace walls. You can use a knife and gouge to do the job but it's just going to take more time and effort.

Remove wood from between the lace walls to a depth of approximately 1/4". I would like to thank the folks at Woodcraft Supply in Parkersburg, West Virginia for providing the Foredom™. When using a bit, burr, or a sanding drum in a drill make sure it is inserted properly and firmly locked in place. You should wear safety glasses or goggles for eye protection when using power equipment.

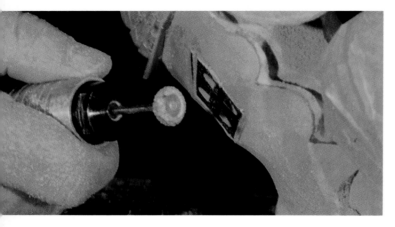

I ran the burr the complete length of the lace wall on both sides. If you have cut the tongue back far enough, you should be able to run the burr right up to the roof eave line. The completed work. Repeat on the other side.

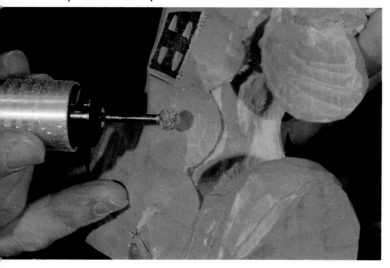

Now use a round burr to clear away any remaining wood.

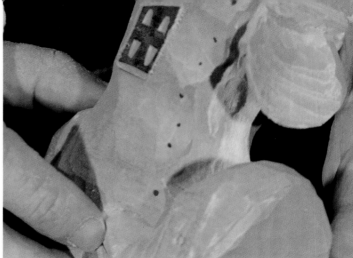

Draw on the holes for the shoe laces. I first place a dot at the top and bottom of the lace wall and then divide the distance and place a dot. I then position two spaced dots between the center dot and the top and bottom dot.

Use a 1/8" drill bit for the holes.

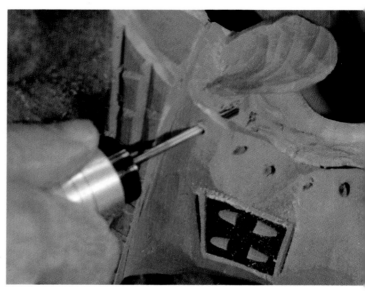

Don't drill straight in! Angle the drill so you can see the bit when it comes through the lace wall.

The finished holes.

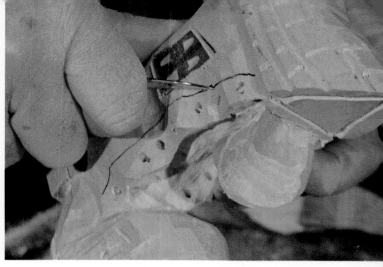

Incise the line. Repeat on the other side.

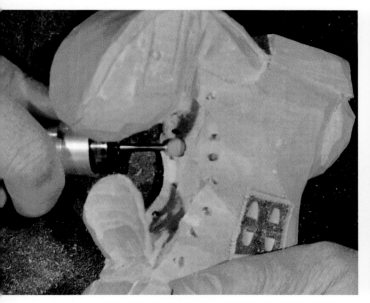

Use a small round burr to clean up between the lace walls. This should make lacing the shoe easier.

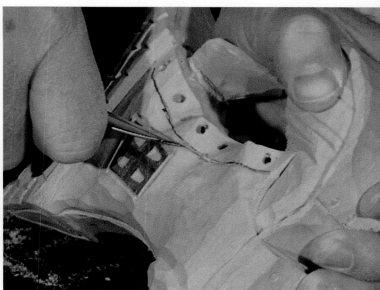

Cut back to the line. Repeat on the other side.

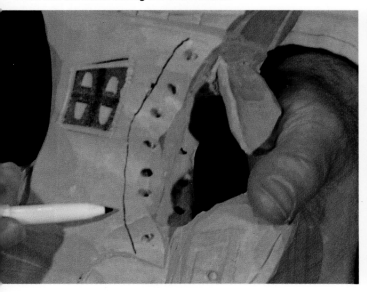

Draw the lace wall seam. Repeat on the other side.

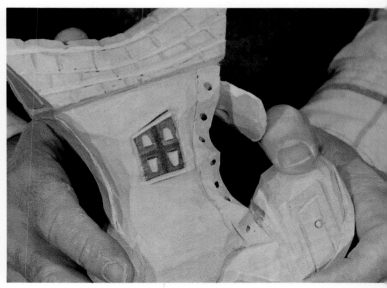

The finished cuts.

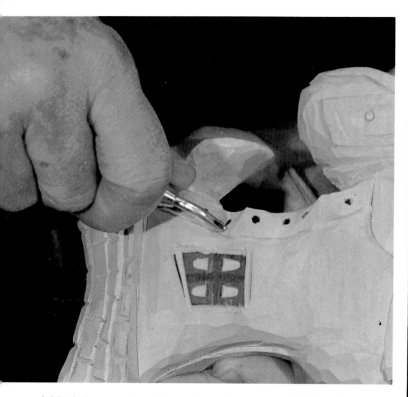

Add stitching marks with a pattern wheel or your knife point on the lace wall seam.

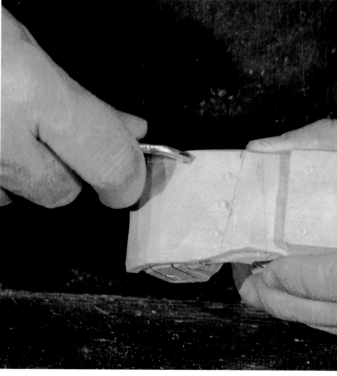

Add stitching marks to the sole.

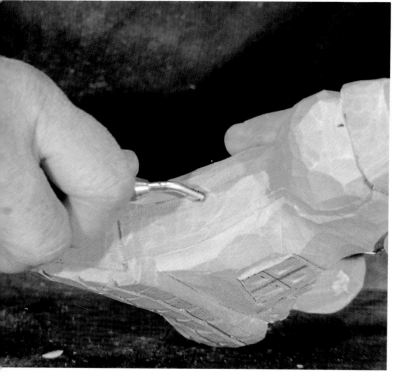

Add stitching marks to the back.

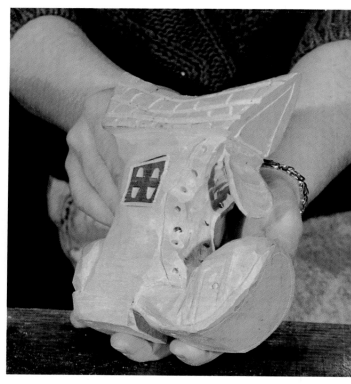

The shoe is ready to be painted. The next sections will show you how to carve the smoke stack, yard, and toothpick flowers.

Carving the Smokestack

Knock off the edges. Round approximately 3" off the block.

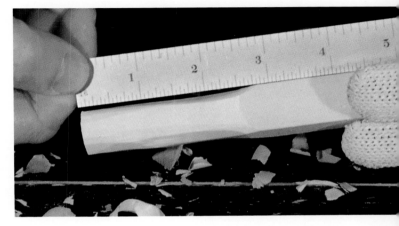

The completed cuts. This should give you plenty of wood with which to work.

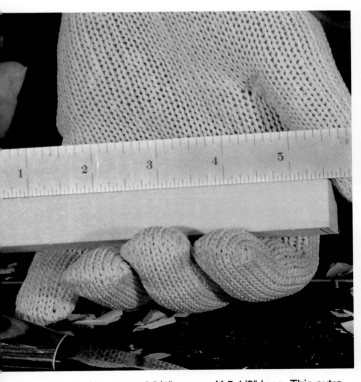

Cut a block of basswood 3/4" square X 5 1/2" long. This extra length will give you some wood for a hand hold while you carve the stack.

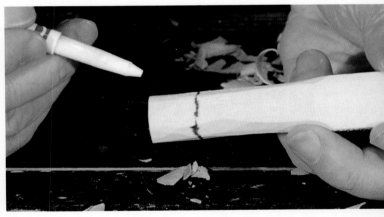

Measure in 3/4" and draw a line completely around the wood.

Make a stop cut on the line completely around the wood.

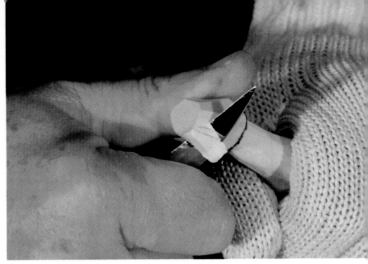

Bring the roof of the stack to a point.

Cut back to the stop cut all the way around. You are working to make the base of the stack smaller.

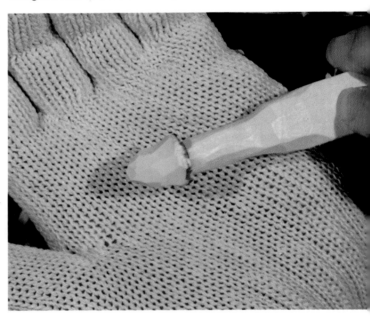

The completed roof of the stack.

The completed cuts. I've cut in just over 1/4" deep.

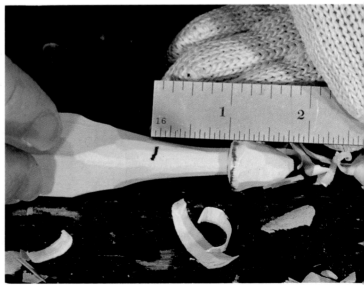

Measure 1" from the base of the stack roof and make a mark.

Use a saw to cut the stack from the block.

The completed stack thus far.

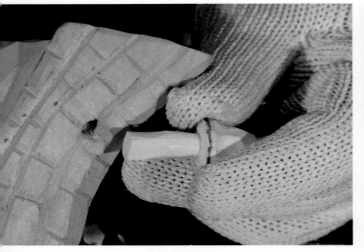

Drill a 1/4" hole in the roof where you want the stack to go. I use a 1/4" size bit because it gives me more control. I then use my knife to ream out the hole a little. Slanting the hole will give the stack a rickety look.

Taper the stack base until it fits into the hole. Place the stack in the hole and rotate it while applying a little pressure. When you remove the stack you will see shiny spots where the base needs trimming.

Repeat this process until you have a good fit.

The roof base of my stack is about 5/8" above the shoe roof. We will attach the stack to the roof later. Lay it aside.

carving the yard

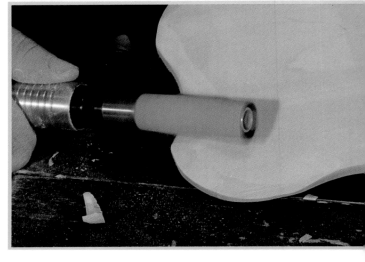

Once you have carved the edges off of the yard and removed any saw marks, use your sand paper or sanding drum to give the yard a good sanding. You can use a sanding drum to add some contour to the edges of the yard.

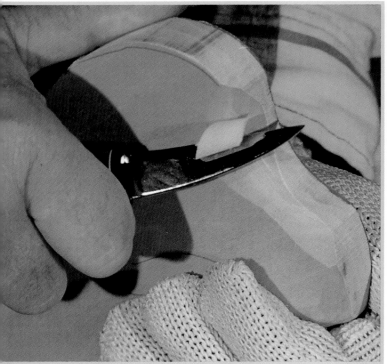

After you have used carbon paper to trace the yard pattern on a 3/4" basswood board, cut the yard out with your band saw and then use your knife to round off the edges.

Place the shoe on the yard and draw the path lines to your liking.

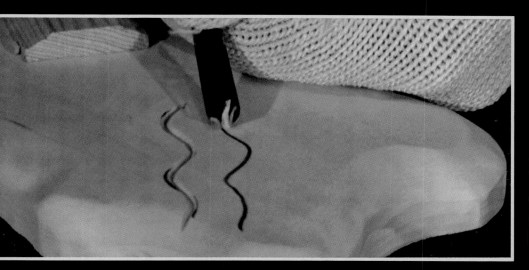

Use a c-clamp to hold the yard and use a v-tool to define the path.

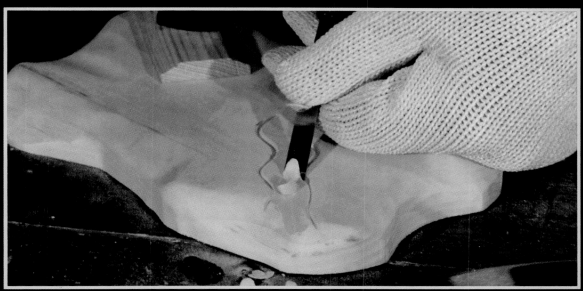

I'm using an 8mm No. 5 gouge to texture and drop the path below the level of the yard.

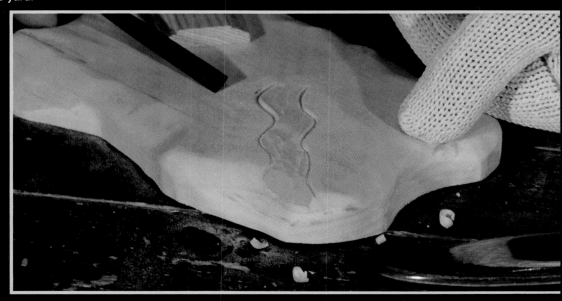

The carved yard with path.

Carving the Flowers

When carving a tooth pick, don't use a lot of pressure or you'll break the pick before you have the flower carved. I'm using an X-acto™ knife with a #11 blade to carve the flowers. If you can find a surgical scalpel with a #11 blade, it will work as well.

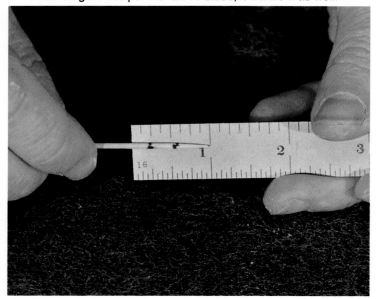

Draw two lines around the tooth pick. Measure in approximately 1/2" for one line and 3/4" inch for the other. You can increase the 3/4" line to 1" and make some larger flowers. To add some variety of size, vary the starting length on some of the flowers. After you have done several flowers, you probably won't need to draw the lines anymore.

Place your knife on the 3/4" line and make a very thin slicing cut toward the 1/2" line. You don't want to dig the knife into the wood. When your knife reaches the 1/2" line, gently roll your knife and the flower petal perpendicular to the shaft of the toothpick. This will help the petal lay away from the shaft.

Rotate the toothpick and make the next cut toward the 1/2" line. One of the keys to carving the flower is to start your knife cut on the 3/4" line and end it at the same place each time. This will take some practice.

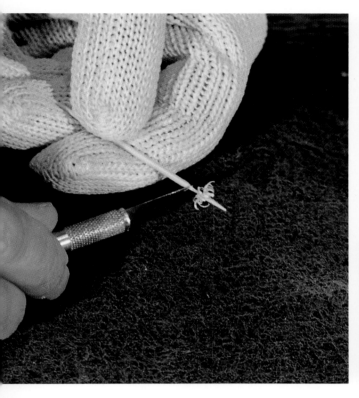

Continue to rotate the tooth pick making cuts around the diameter of the tooth pick until you have finished the flower or it breaks loose. The thinner the cuts, the more times you will be able to "go around" the shaft making petals; the more petals you make the fuller the flower.

I use Ceramcoat™ by Delta acrylic paint straight from the bottle for the flowers.

The completed flower. You will need to make at least 10 - 12 flowers for the path. Don't become discouraged. I had to attempt over 25 flowers to get the 11 needed. It will just take some practice. One thing about carving toothpicks -- the wood is inexpensive!

You can really be creative with painting the flowers. I'm painting my gold, yellow and blue. Set aside and allow to dry.

Finishing the yard

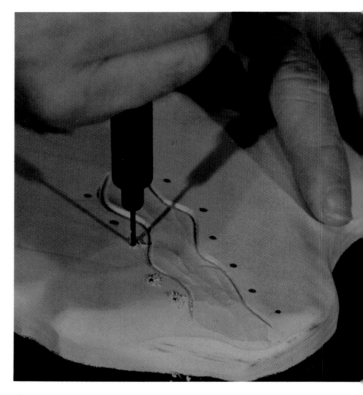

I'm using a 1/16" drill bit to make the holes for the flowers.

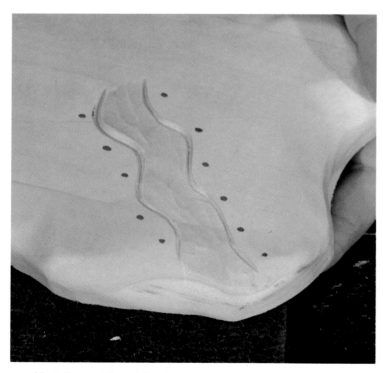

Mark the position of the flowers along the path. You don't need to limit yourself to flowers just along the path. You could make a flower garden in the yard.

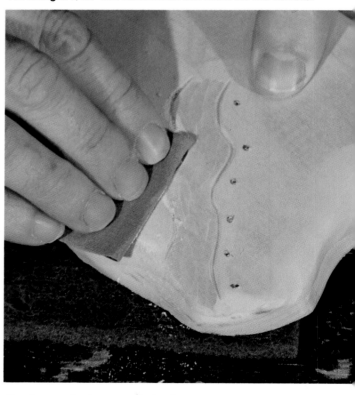

Sand away the burrs made by the drill.

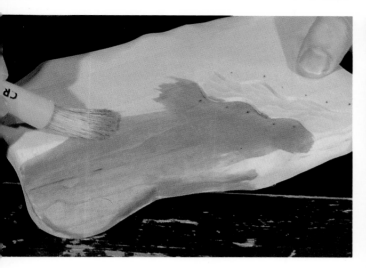

Paint the yard with a wash of Ceramcoat™ by Delta English Yew. Since there are many different greens, you might prefer a different color.

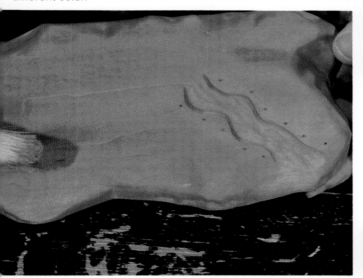

The painted yard.

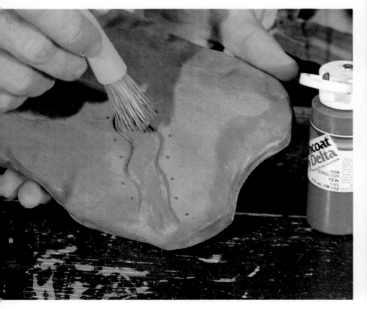

Dab some Autumn Brown paint on the path.

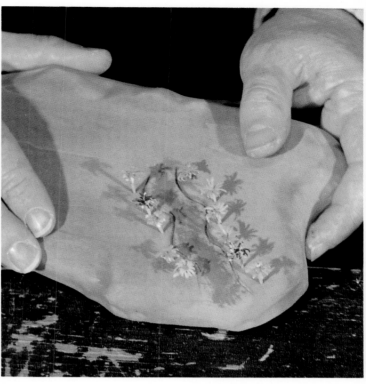

Since I wanted a dull look, I decided not to apply any type of finish to the yard. Allow the yard to dry, then glue in the flowers.

I've placed the shoe on the base just to check everything out.

Painting the Shoe

I finish the shoe in one of three ways. One method is not necessary better than the others.

In all three methods you need to sand the shoe with 220 grit or finer sand paper. The finer the grit the smoother the carving. Using a sanding drum saves time and allows you to sand with the contour of the shoe.

If you use a sanding drum, make sure the drum is in tight and that your wearing some type of eye protection.

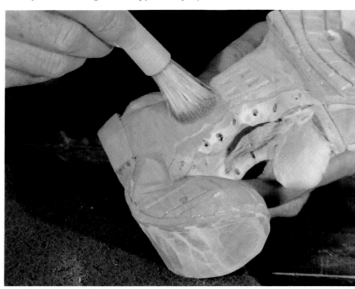

Use a brush to cover the shoe with a light coat of water. This closes the grain and aids in painting. I'm using a Crayola™ So Big Brush™. It's a great brush for covering a lot of area quickly.

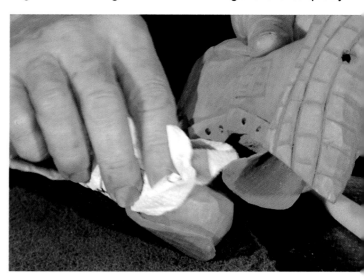

Wipe away any excess water.

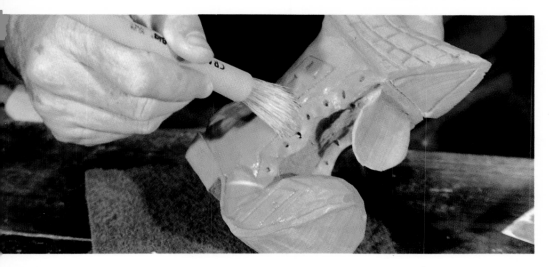

While the shoe is still damp, apply a wash of Ceramcoat™ by Delta Autumn brown paint over the entire shoe.

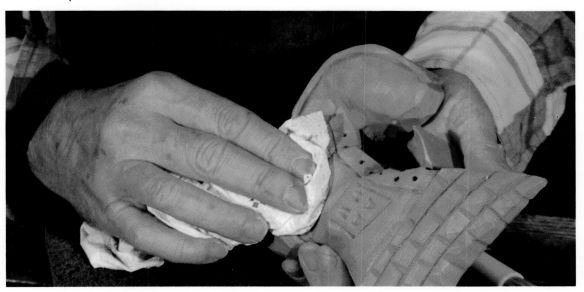

Wipe away any excess paint.

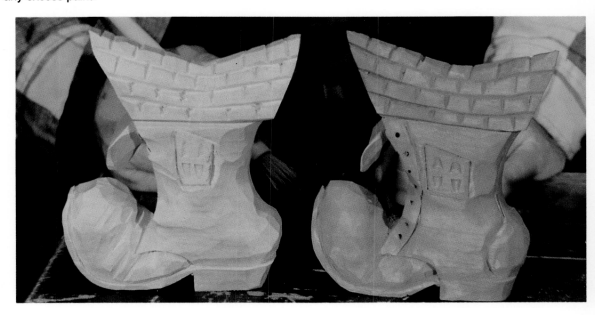

The completed brown wash.

While the shoe is still damp from the brown wash, apply a thick wash of Black Green on the roof.

The result of wiping the roof.

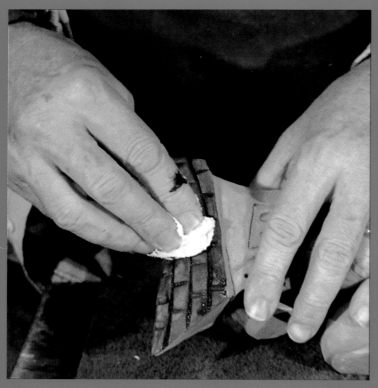

Before the Black Green dries, use a cloth to wipe away some of the paint from the shingles leaving paint in the v-cuts.

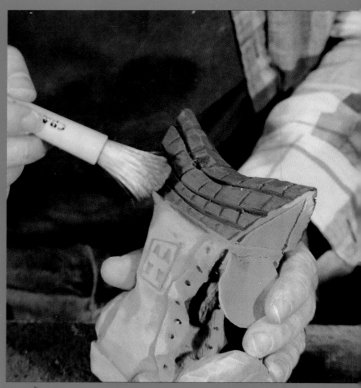

Apply a coat of English Yew on the roof. You want to brush it on so that you don't get a lot of paint into the v-cuts.

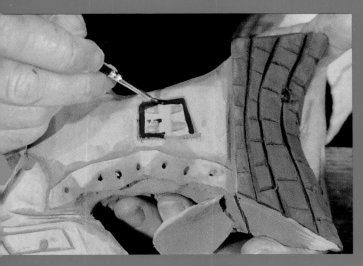

Paint the door and window frame to your liking. I am using blue for the window and door frame.

Paint the window panes with a light yellow. I'm using the paint straight from the bottle.

The finished door and frame. The blue looks dark now but I will tone it down through sanding. You might want to use a lighter color.

Paint the smoke stack black. After the paint is dry, glue the stack in place.

I have painted the door with Bittersweet.

Allow the acrylic paint to dry and then apply a coat of Deft™ Semi-Gloss over all the shoe. Allow to dry.

Use sand paper or a sanding drum to sand away some of the paint. This will give the shoe a worn look.

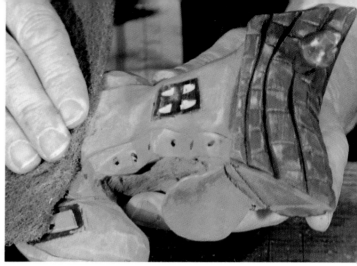

Apply a second coat of Deft™ Semi-Gloss, allow to dry and then use a Scotch-Brite™ pad from some final rubbing. Buff away the dust.

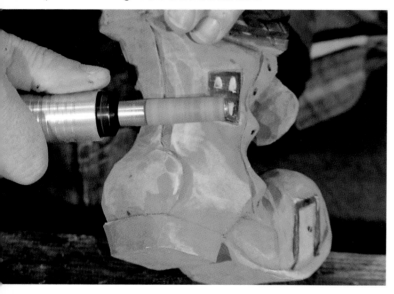

Sand a little, inspect your work, and then sand a little more until you like what you see.

Apply a coat of Minwax™ paste finishing wax over the entire shoe. I use a Crayola™ So Big Brush™ to apply the wax. This allows me to "get" the wax in the v-cuts and those tight spots. Don't use the same brush you paint with to apply the wax.

I like to use a shoe brush to remove dust left through sanding.

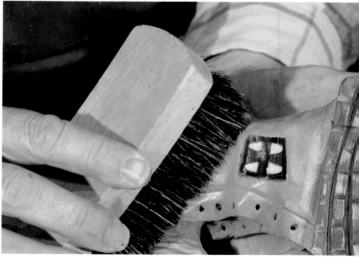

After the wax has dried, buff with a soft cloth or shoe brush.

The painted shoe on the base.

a using 1/8" black leather lace for the shoe string. A pair of
rved tweezers really helps with the lacing job. If you can't
d any lacing, you can cut the laces out of a car chamois. You
n stain it and then lace your shoe.

Use two appropriate sized screws to attach your shoe to the
base.

METHOD 3 for Painting the shoe

1. Sand the shoe with 220 grit or finer paper.
2. Glue in the smoke stack at this time. Allow to dry.
3. Paint the shoe with a wood stain. I like to use Minwax™ Colonial Maple to achieve the color I like. Allow to dry.
4. After the shoe is dry, paint with a coat of Deft™ Semi-Gloss.
5. Follow steps 4 - 7 of Method two.

METHOD 2 for Painting the shoe

1. Sand the shoe with 220 grit or finer paper.
2. Glue in the smoke stack at this time. Allow to dry.
3. Paint the shoe with a coat of Deft™ Semi-Gloss finish.
4. After the Deft™ is dry, sand the shoe with your sand paper or sanding drum. Buff off the dust and repeat with another coat of Deft™.
5. Allow to dry, then give the shoe a light rubbing with a Scotch-Brite™ pad. Buff off the dust.
6. Add a coat of paste wax. I like to use a Crayola™ So Big Brush™ to apply the wax. Using a brush helps you "get" the wax in those tight spots.
7. Allow the wax to dry, then buff with a shoe brush or soft cloth.

*Pattern reduced to **65%**.*
*Enlarge **155%** for original size.*

THE GALLERY

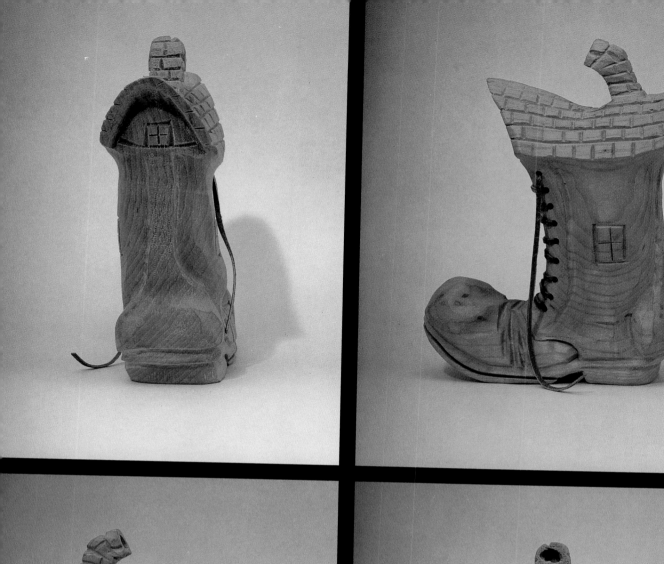